How to Deal With Worry and Anxiety

Simple Mindfulness Techniques to
Relieve Stress and Fear
and Live a Life Without Depression
By: Raymond McGee

Introduction

Anxiety!

   Depression!

   Worry!

   Fear!

The words above represent some of our worst worries in life, and living in an uncertain world doesn't help. That's why there is an increasing discourse on mental health and how to help people combat the impact of fear. This book is timely because it contributes to the conversation about how to deal with worry and anxiety through practical and proven mindfulness techniques.

Yes! You can combat fear with straightforward mindfulness methods. Still, you need to know *how* to achieve this. In this book, we unravel tried and tested ideas that take you from a negative mental state to an empowered one.

What are some of your biggest fears? Why do you stay up at night worrying about the future? Have your worries finally taken over your thought process? Do you struggle to see the silver lining in the cloud? These questions represent the problem we all face (yes "we," because you are not alone).

We need answers and solutions to our common problem, and we will unearth them in the chapters and sections that follow. You will learn the meaning of anxiety, anxiety risk factors, and the symptoms of anxiety. Get ready to discover practical ways of combating fear through mindfulness. This guarantees sustainable results long-term. We will learn about the benefits of mindfulness and how it relates to anxiety. In order to combat fear, we must maximize the use of mindfulness techniques such as breathing exercises, meditation, and other strategies. In this book, the ideas and concepts you will learn will get you out of the mental bondage enabled by fear, thus helping you live a more peaceful life.

Unfortunately, some people quickly give up on the challenge of overcoming fear and anxiety. Fear and anxiety have become woven into the fabric of our dreams and experiences. Worrying is just something that we are comfortable doing and that is easy to do. Some people even start to worry when they don't have something to worry about. This is an especially negative, draining process.

I guarantee that this book will give you access to proven techniques that will empower you with mental skills that set you apart from the millions of people dealing with anxiety daily. Your entire trajectory and potential in life is affected by the impact of anxiety. It affects how you think and what you do. Due to the tremendously negative impact of anxiety and fear on your mental health, you must immediately start to work on overcoming it.

The sooner you start maximizing the value of this book, the sooner you will learn to fight off fear and anxiety. Are you ready for your mental health to undergo a truly transformative change? Let us begin!

Chapter One: What is Anxiety?

When humans encounter a stressful situation, their body and mind are programmed to react in a specific way. One of those reactions is the feeling of anxiety.

The feeling of anxiety is generally unpleasant. It is difficult for an individual to feel calm or at ease when anxious. This is because anxiety affects the whole body and it reacts with both physical and mental symptoms that prevent relaxation. Stress is technically different from anxiety, but the two are closely intertwined. Stress is caused by the demands of an event or scenario that are placed onto an individual's brain or body. Anxiety is the body's reaction to stress and its attempt to cope with the stressful demands it has been presented with. Neither anxiety nor stress are completely negative emotions. Despite their uncomfortable nature, they are a tool that compels an individual to act by providing a boost of motivation or an incentive to accomplish a task or get out of a situation.

Since everyone has experienced stressful situations, it is safe to say that every person has also experienced anxiety at some time in their lives. For anxious feelings to develop, the individual is put under pressure by a situation. This may be a mildly stressful situation such as a job interview, or exam or it may be a highly stressful situation such as amassing lots of debt or being unable to pay rent. The anxiety felt is often proportional to the impact potential of the stressor, and for most people, the anxiety dissipates once the stressful situation has passed.

For most people, feelings of anxiety appear in response to a stressful situation and then disappear. These feelings do not linger longer than they are supposed to and do not interfere with people living their normal lives. Some people, however, have a much harder time controlling feelings of anxiety. The sensation of stress and worry lingers long after a stressor has disappeared. It may even appear without reason when there are no prompts from any stressors at all. Frequent, persistent or extreme feelings of anxiety can interfere with the quality of an individual's daily life. Worrying may begin to affect relationships, work, school and other areas of life. This stage of intense and frequent feelings of anxiety may be indicative of an anxiety disorder, and it is appropriate for suffering individuals to seek help. Left untreated or ignored, victims of extreme anxiety may be at risk of developing depression, suicidal thoughts, substance abuse behaviours and other mental health concerns.

Anxiety disorders are the most common type of mental illness in America. Around 18% of the population are treated each year, and up to 30% of the population will experience a form of anxiety disorder during their lives. Children can also suffer from anxiety disorders. Around 25% of children between 13 and 18 years are negatively affected by anxiety. If anxiety in children isn't treated appropriately, it can lead to more serious issues later in life like depression, drug and alcohol abuse and various neuroses. One reason for the frequency of anxiety disorders is that anxiety has high levels of comorbidity. Anxiety disorders are often diagnosed alongside mental illnesses such as depression, attention deficit

HOW TO DEAL WITH WORRY AND ANXIETY: SIMPLE MINDFULNESS TECHNIQUES TO RELIEVE STRESS AND FEAR AND LIVE A LIFE WITHOUT DEPRESSION

7

hyperactivity disorder (ADHD), and eating disorders such as anorexia and bulimia.

The latest official Diagnostic and Statistical Manual of Mental Disorders, the DSM-5, is the global authority on how anxiety disorders are officially characterized. It considers the main feature of anxiety disorders to be excessive fear that causes a disturbance in behaviour. It separates anxiety disorders into 7 different types.

Generalized Anxiety Disorder (GAD)

Generalized anxiety disorder is a common chronic anxiety disorder. It is a long-term condition with excessive and continuous symptoms of anxiety that rarely diminish. For individuals that suffer from generalized anxiety disorder, almost every day can be plagued with incessant worry and a frustrating inability to control these emotions. Generalized anxiety disorder evokes feelings of anxiety over many daily activities, events and situations and is not limited to 1 situation or event. Anxiety provoking situations range from fears about the future to everyday activities. The level of anxiety felt by the individual is usually wildly disproportionate to the circumstance. This may be to the extent that sufferers are not able to identify the actual source of their anxiety. Generalized anxiety disorder tends to be up to twice as prevalent in women than in men. It is also most commonly found in people between the ages of 35 and 39. The disorder can have detrimental effects on both the mental and physical state of an individual. Very often it occurs along with other anxiety or mental disorders.

Panic Disorder

Panic disorder is expressed by general feelings of anxiety with episodic occurrences of incredibly intense anxiety and terror. These episodes are widely known as panic attacks. They are typically sudden and escalate surprisingly quickly. Victims often reach the peak of the attack within 10 minutes. The rate of de-escalation is varied between different individuals and different situations. It can take between a few minutes to a few hours for the victim of a panic attack to regain control and feel normal. A panic attack is usually unexpected and the majority of them are in response to a trigger. Panic disorders can start to develop after a traumatic or terrifying event in life or after a period of prolonged stress. As a panic attack occurs and escalates, sufferers may feel chest pain, heart palpitations, nausea, shaking and shortness of breath. A panic attack itself can be a scary and traumatic experience for an individual and this can lead to increased worry and anxiety about having another panic attack. Currently, panic disorders affect 2.7% of the American population, and women are twice as likely to be affected as men.

Specific Phobias

Phobias can be an intense and life changing source of anxiety. Specific phobia anxiety disorders are overwhelmingly due to an irrational fear of a particular object or situation that would be deemed non-frightening or even safe by others. Examples of specific phobias include a fear of heights, dogs, blood, enclosed places, and going to school, among many others. The direct cause is not exactly known but they are suspected to be caused by a traumatic event early in life. Even when individuals afflicted by a specific phobia are able to acknowledge the irrational nature of their phobia, they are unable to control the feelings of fear and anxiety when confronted with the object of their phobia. When an individual is exposed to their phobia, they are likely to exhibit signs of fear and make an attempt to get away. In extreme cases, sufferers may even have a panic attack when their specific phobia is present. When the phobia is not present, individuals will still have anxiety surrounding the phobia. They will go out of their way to avoid coming into contact with their phobia, even when it is detrimental to the flow of their everyday life. Specific phobias, in varying degrees of intensity, affect 8.7% of the American population.

Agoraphobia

Individuals afflicted with agoraphobia get excessive feelings of anxiety about particular places, events or situations. Typically, agoraphobia can present as either a fear of large open spaces or a fear of enclosed spaces. This fear is propelled by the belief that these places would be difficult to escape from if needed, or conversely, that the person is only safe in their home. A person with agoraphobia may be afraid of elevators, buses, airplanes, large crowds and movie theatres. This is because they are enclosed or crowded spaces that they would be concerned about getting trapped inside. Alternatively, they may be fearful of large, open spaces, or of being outside of their home. When individuals with agoraphobia find themselves in an uncomfortable situation and location, they will begin to experience intense anxiety symptoms and may begin to panic. To prevent these terrifying feelings from occurring, sufferers of agoraphobia often make extreme changes to their lifestyle to avoid triggering situations. They may refuse to go certain places, or may sometimes refuse to leave the house for weeks at a time. Less than 1% of the US population suffers from agoraphobia, but women are more likely to experience it than men.

Selective Mutism

Selective mutism is most commonly found in children, however, if left untreated it can persist into teenage years and even adulthood. It is a form of anxiety in which children are unable to speak in certain situations, even when they are able to communicate effectively in other situations. A common situation where selective mutism arises is when children first start going to school. Although they are able to speak sufficiently in the comfort of their own home, they are unable to verbally communicate at school. Selective mutism is suspected to be an extreme form of social phobia and it can have a negative impact on the social development and functioning of the children or adults it targets.

Social Anxiety Disorder

Social anxiety disorder is characterized by high levels of anxiety and fear when confronted with the prospect of social situations. These feelings are based on self-consciousness and a fear of judgement by others. Individuals with social anxiety will be unable to enjoy social situations as they will be experiencing symptoms of anxiety like dizziness, nausea, and a racing heart. They will be worried about what to say, how to act and how they will be perceived. As a result of these fears, people with social anxiety will say and do the minimal amount in social situations, and are therefore often perceived as shy and quiet. Social anxiety disorder may also present as a fear of intimacy as the individual will attempt to avoid vulnerable situations where humiliation or rejection may be an outcome. In extreme cases, individuals with social anxiety will attempt to avoid human interaction altogether, to the extent that it affects their daily routine, work, school and relationships.

Separation Anxiety Disorder

People of any age can suffer from separation anxiety disorder, although it is most commonly found in children. Those with separation anxiety disorder experience excessive anxiety when separated from people or a place that is important to them and with which they have a strong emotional attachment. For children this is often the home environment, adults, siblings or another primary care figure. In adults, feelings of anxiety can occur when separated from the home environment, a loved one or significant other. Separation anxiety disorder is thought to be caused by a loss of a source of security and safety. The act of separation can spark feelings of anxiety that range from mild to severe and can even result in a panic attack. Separation anxiety disorder affects around 15% of the U.S. population.

The DSM also includes Obsessive Compulsive Disorder (OCD) which consists of irrational or intrusive thoughts that result in the repetition of specific behaviours, and Post-Traumatic Stress Disorder (PTSD) which involves heightened anxiety following a traumatic event. In the most recent edition of the DSM, these mental health issues are no longer included under the category of anxiety, but have been moved to other categories.

Although mostly described as a symptom of anxiety, panic attacks warrant their own definition. They are similar to panic disorder, but not the same. A panic attack can be a response to a known trigger or it can occur spontaneously without a clear source. They occur suddenly and reach their peak within minutes, often involving intense and overwhelming feelings of terror and anxiety. Panic attacks are accompanied by frightening physical symptoms such as nausea, a racing heartbeat, dizziness and shortness of breath. Panic attacks can happen to anyone, but many or frequent attacks can be signs of panic disorder.

Unlike panic attacks, anxiety attacks are not validated by the DSM-5. The unofficial phenotype of an anxiety attack shares similar qualities to panic attacks, but are not identical. An anxiety attack is a feeling of overwhelming apprehension, worry, distress or fear. Generally, anxiety builds slowly and worsens as a stressful event approaches. One of the reasons that an anxiety attack is not officially recognized is because there is a lot of variation in the presentation and experience of an anxiety attack. Symptoms can differ drastically among individuals and over time.

In the next chapter, we will discuss anxiety risk factors to help you understand where anxiety comes from, and what contributes to it.

Chapter Two: Anxiety Risk Factors

Research has uncovered a range of potential risk factors that can explain why individuals develop an anxiety disorder. Both nature and nurture are relevant inputs into the range of risk factors which come from neurobiological sources, environmental factors and life experiences. People who suffer from an anxiety disorder may have a single risk factor, multiple risk factors or none. It is not yet fully understood what causes some people to develop anxiety disorders, or why many people experience these disorders for no apparent reason.

Comorbidity, or the presence of two chronic conditions simultaneously, is very common with regard to anxiety disorders. Individuals that experience one type of anxiety disorder are likely to also develop another. Some risk factors are unique to a particular type of anxiety disorder but most risk factors are shared across the spectrum of anxiety disorders. It is possible that an individual has a risk factor or multiple factors and will never develop an anxiety disorder. It is, however, useful to understand risk factors so that support and assistance can be provided to those at risk.

Genetic Risk Factors

Overall, anxiety disorders have a heritability rate of up to 67%. This means that they tend to run in families and the biological factors that lead to the development of an anxiety disorder are likely to be inherited. While the heritability rate wavers slightly for individual anxiety disorders, inheritance has been documented for each of them. The "biological factors" that can increase the risk of anxiety refers to a selection of single nucleotide polymorphisms (SNPs) that are present in the section of the genetic code involved in the expression and regulation of stress hormones and neurotransmitter systems. These SNPs are passed on through the DNA and those with a close relative that suffers from an anxiety disorder can be up to 5 times more likely to develop an anxiety disorder. Genetic factors can also work in the opposite direction and increase resilience to anxiety disorders. It is also important to remember that the inheritance of genetic risk factors for anxiety disorders does not guarantee that they will develop.

Environmental Risk Factors

There are a number of environmental risk factors that can lead someone to develop an anxiety disorder either while young or later in life. Parental behaviour has a dramatic effect on the wellbeing of children, particularly regarding their mental health. Parenting that involves excessive levels of control without giving children the chance to be independent or autonomous is a risk factor for that child to develop an anxiety disorder. Contrarily, children that perceived parental rejection are also at a greater risk of developing an anxiety disorder. Additionally, parents that exhibit anxious behaviours themselves risk their behaviour rubbing off on the child who will likely grow up to demonstrate similar anxious behaviours.

Stressful events that occur in childhood cause a child to have a greater risk of developing an anxiety disorder. If a child experiences or witnesses trauma, experiences bullying, sexual, physical or emotional abuse, domestic violence or the loss of a parent, they are much more likely to experience anxiety throughout their teenage and adult years and may develop an anxiety disorder..

Medical Conditions

Anxiety can be a symptom of many medical conditions. It is not uncommon for health care providers to check for underlying health problems in patients that suffer from anxiety. Some medical conditions that are risk factors for the development of anxiety include thyroid disease, menopause, diabetes, heart disease and some tumours that affect stress hormone production. Additionally, difficulties with insomnia, falling asleep or staying asleep can also lead to increased levels of anxiety.

Although not directly causal, suffering or being diagnosed with any illness or medical condition can cause anxiety, especially if it is long-term or painful. Worry and stress over maintaining one's health, particularly when ill, can lead to intense anxiety that can develop into a disorder. The health of family members or close friends can also lead to high levels of anxiety that can have an effect on daily life.

Behavioural Choices

An individual's choices could greatly increase the risk of developing an anxiety disorder. Excessive intake of tobacco and caffeine have been shown to be risk factors for increased anxiety. Alcohol and drug use, abuse and withdrawal can cause or exacerbate the development of an anxiety disorder. Even though the use of drugs such as alcohol and cannabis can be relaxing in the short term, long term use can increase feelings of anxiety and lead to an anxiety disorder. Behavioural choices can also decrease the risk of developing an anxiety disorder. A healthy diet and regular exercise can both significantly reduce the impact of anxiety.

Gender

Females have a much higher risk of developing an anxiety disorder than males. The fluctuation of ovarian hormones such as progesterone and oestrogen are implicated in the increased severity and prevalence of symptoms of anxiety in women.

Chapter Three: Symptoms and Effects of Anxiety

Anxiety is how the body responds to danger. It is an evolutionary tool that sets off a chain of events both physically and mentally that prepares the body to run away or fight. In the event of danger, the hormones adrenaline and cortisol are released, among others. They flow through the blood and quickly reach the far corners of the body and brain to make the changes that give the individual the best chances of survival. However, this is supposed to be a temporary fix that allows the individual to escape and then return to normal. Anxiety disorders result in a heightened and frequent level of stress. A constant state of anxiety and frequent release of hormones such as adrenaline and cortisol can have long term negative effects on physical and mental health.

There are a wide range of symptoms that anxiety can evoke. An individual may feel all, some, or one of these symptoms, and symptoms vary both between individuals and between situations. People with anxiety disorders experience these symptoms much more often and have trouble controlling them.

Typical examples of the symptoms of anxiety include:

Cardiovascular Effects

During periods of anxiety, an individual is likely to experience an increased heart rate. They may also have heart palpitations and chest pain. These symptoms are generally due to the release of adrenalin and are thought to evolve from the necessity to meet the demands on the body during times of danger. A faster heart rate means quicker delivery of oxygen to muscles which can aid in the fight or flight response. Experiencing a rapid heart rate frequently can put people at an increased risk of high blood pressure and heart disease.

Respiratory Effects

Hyperventilation and shortness of breath are common symptoms of anxiety. Similar to a rapid heartbeat, the body is reacting to perceived danger by breathing rapidly to move more oxygen through the lungs and around the body. However, these actions can feel like there isn't enough oxygen being absorbed in the body, which can in turn cause more anxiety and panic.

Feeling Restless or Worried

One of the main symptoms of anxiety is excessive worrying and an accompanying feeling of restlessness. For people with an anxiety disorder, the amount of worry is often largely out of proportion to the events that trigger it. Indeed, it is often unremarkable, everyday events that prompt bouts of worry.

Difficulty Sleeping

Sleep disturbances can cause an increase in anxiety, and anxiety can cause sleep disturbances. While it is not clear in each individual's case which came first, treatments of anxiety often lead to improvement of sleep quality and better sleeping patterns. Naturally, long term sleep deprivation can lead to further health problems including depression, loss of brain function, cardiovascular problems, a weakened immune system and psychiatric disorders. Inability to sleep is the body's attempt at keeping you awake and alert so you can react in the event of danger.

Tense Muscles

People with anxiety might find that they are frequently tensing their muscles throughout the day. Although muscle tensing is caused by feelings of anxiety, engaging in therapeutic techniques to relax muscles also results in a reduction in feelings of anxiety. It's suspected that tense muscles are a tool the body uses to help prepare to get away from danger quickly. Unfortunately, muscle tensing can result in pain, tension headaches and migraines.

Fatigue

Fatigue may be a surprising symptom of anxiety, since it is usually associated with being on edge. However, many sufferers of anxiety disorders find they often feel fatigued. Fatigue can be chronic, frequently occurring without any prompt, however, it often occurs after a panic attack. Other symptoms like sleeping difficulties or muscle tensing may be linked to fatigue and there is also the possibility that fatigue is a symptom of a comorbid condition such as depression.

Panic Attacks

The overwhelming fear arising from a panic attack comes on within minutes and is accompanied by many extreme symptoms of anxiety including heart palpitations, excessive sweating, noticeable shaking or trembling, chest pains, dizziness and shortness of breath. A panic attack can happen in isolation or can occur frequently and unexpectedly. Frequent panic attacks are symptomatic of panic disorder.

Digestive System

Anxiety can have significant effects on the digestive and excretory systems. When the body perceives danger, it draws the blood away from the digestive system and towards muscles in case of the need to run or fight. This can result in stomach aches, diarrhoea, nausea and loss of appetite.

Chapter Four: Mindfulness

Keeping up with the modern world demands busy days, completing errands, working, multitasking, supervising and running around hectically to stay on top of responsibilities. In this rush of fulfilling tasks and crossing off to-do lists, many people are missing out on experiencing their lives. They pass up the opportunity to reflect on where they are and what they are doing, and moments disappear in a blur. Without connection to the present moment, individuals feel ungrounded, lost and unsure.

Loss of connection to the present moment often results in spending too much time away from our bodies and living in our heads, ruminating on the past or worrying about the future. Remembering and analyzing the past is a useful activity as it can help us learn from our previous actions and improve in future scenarios. Equally, thinking about the future can help develop goals and set up plans for reaching them. However, too much of either can be maladaptive. Our minds can be in a different time and place from our bodies, engrossed in harmful, negative, repetitive thinking patterns that can lead to anxiety, depression and damaging behaviours.

Mindfulness is an active mental state of being aware of the present moment. It is knowing what you are experiencing in each moment both on the inside of oneself and in your outside surroundings. Experiencing your internal self includes paying attention to your own thoughts, feelings and emotions without judgement. Mindfulness is a tool that gives you access to your emotions without being shackled to them. Subsequently, you'll be better equipped to identify emotions, you will be able to experience them more fully, and you'll be able to process emotions in a healthy manner that is more reflective than reactive.

Additionally, mindfulness enables you to consider new perspectives. Altercations and confrontations can result in negative feelings on both sides of the argument. Instead of being blinded by personal reactionary emotions, mindfulness can provide access to the full picture. It can be easier to understand that the person on the other side may be feeling stressed, tired or upset and their discontent may not be personal. By allowing space to consider a mindful perspective, negative feelings can be understood, experienced and alleviated.

External experiences include the purposeful attentiveness to current activities and the sensory input that is being received. When mindful, we are fully present and engaged in the current moment without surrendering to distraction from thoughts and emotions. The self reconnects to the physical body and focuses on the sensations it experiences by actively noticing the sights, sounds, tastes and textures of the present moment. You are purposefully engaging in your existence.

Mindfulness is innate for each person. It is not an unreachable goal, a transient fad or a competition. Instead, it is a universally available natural quality that simply needs to be accessed and applied. Everyone has the capacity for mindfulness and can begin the practice of mindfulness at any moment. In fact, there are many times during a week or even during a day that individuals are being mindful without knowing that's what they are doing. Mindfulness can be applied at any time of the day during any activity, as it is the act of creating space to think, to notice and to experience the present moment of being.

Actively working towards mindfulness doesn't require a change of goals, beliefs, personality or lifestyle. Options that demand a change of an individual's core beliefs or identity will inevitably result in failure. Mindfulness works with what is already there. It amplifies the best within each person while giving them tools to continue their growth. Not only do mindful individuals have a more comprehensive understanding of themselves, they are able to enjoy life more.

How Mindfulness Works

Mindfulness can liberate an individual from enslavement by their own thoughts and emotions by paying attention to them and to external surroundings. Instead of disappearing into the mind to focus on things that have already happened or on things that might happen, mindfulness empowers people to be aware of their emotions while remaining focused on the present.

This stops emotions from becoming overwhelming by keeping it at a respectable distance. As emotions are no longer in charge, more rational and reflective responses can be formed.

Preparing for Your Mindfulness Practice

Mindfulness is easy for anyone to learn and apply. It is an accessible tool that is completely free to use and implement and can be practiced anywhere at any time. Mindfulness doesn't require any special equipment or clothing. However, there are certain aspects to be aware of before beginning the practice.

Converse to popular presumptions about mindfulness, the goal is not to clear the mind. Attempts to achieve an empty mind, void of thoughts and focus are unlikely to succeed. This can lead to frustration and a disillusionment with the practice of mindfulness. Instead, the aim of mindfulness is to focus the mind on the present moment. Although this can also take some practice, it is much easier to achieve than a clear mind.

Practitioners of mindfulness will find that the mind frequently wanders. This is expected and should not be taken as a sign of failure or inability to perfect the skill. Some estimates say that the human mind spends up to half of its awake-time wandering. Positive mind-wandering can be a pleasant activity and can increase creativity in individuals. However, negative mind wandering often results in rumination and worry. Naturally, frequent habits of mind wandering can be difficult to control at first, particularly as we often don't even realize our mind is wandering.

Mindfulness is the ability to notice that the mind has wandered and to purposefully bring it back to the present moment. As mindfulness is practiced, individuals will be able to recognize a wandering mind more quickly and will find it increasingly easy to both refocus the mind on the present moment and to stay in the present moment.

Chapter Five: Mindfulness and Anxiety

Rumination is the act of repeatedly thinking about a specific situation, event, or problem without finding an acceptable solution. The object of rumination could be something that occurred in the past, or something that occurs in the present or might happen in the future. The repetition in the mind of the issue without finding a solution can cause feelings of anxiety, which leads to further rumination and increased stress levels, which are detrimental to finding a solution.

Anxiety is often misplaced. The reason that a solution to ruminating thoughts can't be found is that anxious thoughts focus on the things that have happened and can't be changed or have not yet happened. Anxiety inducing ruminations tends to present as replaying the same past scenario repeatedly, focusing on things that could have been handled differently or what you wish had never happened. These factors can never be changed and they are not conducive to improving the situation.

Thinking about tomorrow helps us make plans and work towards goals. We can think about the consequences we wish to avoid, which can guide the actions we take. However, when the mind begins to ruminate on potential future events, anxiety, and stress levels increase. This can decrease the rational ability to make effective decisions in the present that serve to avoid unwanted outcomes.

While it is normal for people to think about the future and ponder how their current actions or inactions contribute to their overall goals, when these thoughts continue on an excessive scale, they become a challenge. The challenge is encapsulated in the word "anxiety."

When thinking about anxiety and mindfulness, hold on to these two words: reflective and reactive, as they will provide insight into the connection between both concepts.

Anxiety makes a person reactive. You will suddenly react to everything happening around and within you with fear because you have conjured up the worst-case scenario. The mind responds to anxiety caused by increased stress levels, which makes the person feel restless, affecting their ability to make logical decisions.

When anxiety is not controlled or left unchecked, it can lead to serious mental complications and prevent people from living to their true potential. This is because fear has a devastating impact on the mind. A person who reacts with fear at every scary news story or negative situation will always live with anxiety. To counter the impact of anxiety on the mind, you can use mindfulness, which enables reflection instead reactionary measures.

With mindfulness, we are encouraged to reflect on situations through a calm mental state. Instead of reacting to every case, we cultivate non-judgmental awareness that helps us distance ourselves from our thoughts and feelings. If we remain in the realms of reaction enabled by anxiety, we will often label our thoughts and feelings "good or bad," which causes a high level of mental stress.

On the contrary, with mindfulness, you are not looking for what is "good or bad". Instead, you separate yourself from the thoughts and only consider the situation for what it is (an isolated situation and not one that affects how you think).

When you maximize the reactive and reflective approach, it becomes easy to understand why mindfulness and anxiety are two ideas that are considered together. This is because one reduces the impact that the other has on a person's mind.

While anxiety compels your thoughts to focus on the future and become afraid of what might happen based on previous experiences, mindfulness helps you focus on the present moment. With mindfulness, it becomes easier to counter rumination and worry. You would be empowered to avoid worrying about tomorrow or ruminating about the past.

Instead of thinking things like, "How am I going to pay my bills next year?" and "I wish I had done things better in my teens", you hold on to the power of the present and live in that moment. However, living in the moment through mindfulness doesn't mean you completely ignore the realities of your life, refuse to learn from your past mistakes, or fail to plan for your future.

Mindfulness helps you stay present enough to hold on to the truth of the moment without fear. Without fear, you will achieve your goals, live a peaceful life, and bask in the feeling of a balanced mindset. While we plan for the future and learn from the past, mindfulness reminds us not to spend much time outside of the present moment, since when we do this we become depressed and anxious.

Research has shown that mindfulness aids in reducing anxiety and depression, because it teaches people how to respond to stress with a sense of awareness instead of reacting to it with fear. Fear is one of the biggest anxiety triggers, and it makes people act instinctively while being unconscious of the fact that their emotions or motives heavily influence their actions.

But the challenge of anxiety can be combated with mindfulness when you are encouraged to open up to your emotions by accepting them instead of being frightful or suspicious of them. Some people quickly become anxious because growing up and in their adult life, they were never taught how to manage their emotions.

Emotional management entails identifying the emotion, experiencing it, and processing it, which is what mindfulness teaches you. Still, anxiety encourages you to view the feeling as a threat to your peace. How do you react to threats? You respond to threats through fear because you are worried the idea or thing might hurt you.

Sadly this fear of emotions is one reason why so many people are neck-deep into depression. For example, if your boss snaps at you at the office, you may worry that you did something wrong to get them upset. If you persistently fear the event happening again, it will influence your mood and cause you to feel incompetent.

However, with mindfulness, you are trained to distance yourself from an immediate response by analyzing the situation logically instead of emotionally. Mindfulness helps you realize that there are other reasons why your boss is upset. Maybe he has had a long day or has family challenges. Regardless of what it may be, it is not about you!

Giving new interpretations to situations that upset you and make you worry can help you avoid anxious experiences, and that is how mindfulness works. This "new" interpretation will help you have a more realistic analysis of the situation, and it also enables body awareness, which we will discuss more in Chapter Ten).

Mindfulness also reduces anxiety through focused attention. By focusing your attention on the present moment, it will become increasingly difficult for you to worry about something else. Your level of self-perception also changes as you no longer see your experiences as static.

Viewing one's life through static lenses makes it easier for a person to worry over everything because they subconsciously believe that whatever happens will hurt them permanently. They start to think that they cannot handle the past or influence the future.

When a person views life's events as temporary and through the lenses of the present, encouraged by mindfulness, every incident is seen as an "ongoing" as opposed to being "final". You will no longer feel trapped in your mind about what to do with future expectations, and neither will you feel powerless about the past.

There is so much to say about the connection between mindfulness and anxiety that if we continue to expand on its related concepts, we may never tackle the other aspects of the discourse in subsequent chapters. The key takeaway is this: you can combat anxiety through mindfulness.

If someone is trapped in the past, unaware of the present and frightful of the future, they will be prone to anxiety and depression. Through mindfulness, answers and solutions become more accessible for people, thus they can avoid the pitfall of fear. This is achieved through the proven methods and techniques we will discuss in Chapter Seven.

Here, we have introduced the concept of mindfulness and how it relates to anxiety. We considered the connection between two key ideas that represent what we must avoid (reactions) and what we must embrace (reflective). While this chapter asserts that it is okay to plan for the future and learn from the past, we should remember to hold on to the present moment because mindfulness is how we can combat anxiety.

Moving on from here, we will now build on the information in this chapter by providing details about the benefits of mindfulness. Why should you take mindfulness seriously, and what does anyone stand to gain with this practice? Aside from the value of mindfulness discussed in this chapter, are there other additional benefits? Proceed to the next chapter to find out more.

Chapter Six: The Other Benefits of Mindfulness

In the previous chapter, we discovered the connection between mindfulness and anxiety while paying attention to their symbiotic relationship (one affects the other). However, there are additional benefits of mindfulness you should know about. This will help you realize just how important it is in helping you curtail the impact of worry and anxiety.

In this chapter, we will explore some specific and impactful benefits of mindfulness. These benefits of mindfulness impact physical, mental, and emotional health. Here we will present 10 of the most commonly reported benefits.

Less Emotional Reactivity

Emotional reactivity is a leading cause of worry and fear in people. The more a person reacts emotionally to specific situations, the easier it becomes for them to feel mental stress.

Mindfulness enables calm and peace within one's mind such that emotional reactivity is reduced, and the individual handles issues from a position of clarity. Do you recall when we talked about being reactive and how it affects your mental state?

The more reactive a person is, the higher the propensity for them to become worried and anxious. Through mindfulness techniques, it is easy to lessen emotional reactions such that instead of being reactive, we become more relaxed and logical.

Cognitive Flexibility

In addition to helping people become less reactive, mindfulness also ensures greater cognitive flexibility. A study discovered that people who are intentional with mindfulness develop better flexible cognitive skills that help them handle situations more effectively.

For example, with mindfulness skills such as meditation, a person achieves mental strength, which is a significant cognitive booster. Mindfulness enables clarity, reduces distractions, and enables critical thinking.

Reduces and Treats Depression

Mindfulness reduces the impact of depression and is a suitable treatment as well. Anyone who is depressed or has experienced depressive episodes can find solace in the healing possibilities of mindfulness. A person who intentionally practices mindfulness is less susceptible to depression and will enjoy a healthier relationship with themself and others.

Depression doesn't happen in isolation. It occurs after a series of events that build up to an imbalanced mental headspace, but mindfulness combats these experiences.

Mindfulness Banishes Temporary Negative Feelings

Bitterness, anger, regret, pain (go on, add more words that depict negative emotions to this list). All of these feelings build up to anxiety and depression. If they are left unchecked, it can affect an individual's mental health long-term. Although these are "temporary" feelings, they can cause enough extensive damage that it cripples a person's mental state.

Moreover, such feelings enable fear, and the best way to prevent its continuous impact is by utilizing mindfulness techniques. Instead of sitting all day dealing with anxiety and concern over the future of your career, mindfulness helps you enjoy the moment and gives your best to the present time.

Stress Reduction

Stress is a trigger for anxiety, and one of the benefits of mindfulness is that it aids the reduction of stress. Imagine having a challenging day and feeling the pressure ebbing slowly out of your body. Mindfulness helps individuals relax. Stress that is usually associated with specific events does not get to them. Techniques such as meditation and yoga, which we will discuss at length in later chapters, help keep an individual mentally balanced enough to keep pressure away.

Prevents Depression Relapse

People who deal with depression sometimes find ways to get out of it, but being depression-free requires you to ensure a decline doesn't happen. Research-based on mindfulness-based cognitive therapy proves that mindfulness prevents depression relapse.

Patients with depression and patients with a history of major depressive disorder who actively engage in mindfulness practices build a robust mental resilience that protects them from future relapse. The assurance of not experiencing a decline is derived from the fact that through techniques such as yoga, meditation, and body awareness, patients take better control of their minds and are less receptive to depressive thoughts.

Mindfulness Reduces Distractions in the Brain

Through mindfulness, you can train your mind to focus on specific tasks, thus reducing distractions and other inconsistencies in the brain. It is easy to become distracted in the world we live in because of the vast array of digital materials and different things that compete for our attention.

However, the times you spend being mindful and staying present in the moment helps you quieten the brain such that you only give attention to the things that matter as opposed to being distracted all the time.

Life and Relationship Satisfaction

Another benefit of mindfulness is the satisfaction you enjoy with your life and relationships because it helps you become more conscious of the joys in your life. A mindful person is also a grateful one who doesn't complain about negative experiences in life but finds satisfaction in the good they see and experience.

Through consistent mindful engagements, such people become more conscious of their valuable relationships and are more content with their lives.

Better Sleep

One of the most harmful impacts of worry and anxiety is that it robs you of proper sleep. While others sleep, depressed and anxious people toss and turn at night because they have so much on their minds that they can't fall asleep or stay asleep.

However, if you practice mindfulness long enough, you will observe changes in your sleep quality and cycles such that you enjoy restful nights. You have poor sleep patterns because you are not living in the present moment, and you allow worries of the future or the past to steal your present-day consciousness. Mindfulness corrects this vicious cycle by increasing your awareness of the NOW and finding contentment at that moment.

Improves Attention

Mindfulness is a proven technique that enhances an individual's ability to sustain a better attention span. Some people are unable to concentrate on a particular task or life event, and this lack of concentration contributes to a lack of confidence in their abilities to get things done.

When a person is not as confident as they should be, their tendency to become anxious increases. This is when mindfulness becomes a crucial technique to use. When a person starts practicing several mindfulness skills, they will experience an improved attention span with an increased ability to pay attention without distractions.

Mindfulness is a viable, efficient technique to empower you to overcome your anxiety. You are mentally capable of handling anything that threatens your peace with worry and anxiety. How can we use mindfulness to address the stresses we face? Are there specific skills we can learn to get the best out of this technique? From Chapter Eight to Ten, we will extensively detail the various types of mindfulness techniques you can implement to deal with worry, combat fear, and eliminate anxiety. Get ready to learn skills you can use right away to help you keep anxiety at bay!

Chapter Seven: Mindfulness Techniques: Breathing Exercises

Breathing exercises are the first mindfulness technique you need to learn. Although breathing is a fundamental process, this technique enables you to focus the pace and flow of your breathing such that it impacts your state of mind. Breathing exercises also help you to focus and feel each inhale and exhale of breath. This allows you to turn your attention away from anxious feelings, fear, and negative emotions.

Through mindfulness breathing techniques, you can harness your breath's power by being grounded in the present moment, thus reestablishing inner calm. As opposed to being overwhelmed by everything happening around you, you feel a sense of relief and peace when your attention is no longer on the issues, but on how you breathe.

Breathing techniques explain why people feel better after mindfulness exercises. Through inhaling and exhaling, a person releases negative energies and breaths in calm energy that combats fear.

In that calm moment, nothing disturbs your peace. The oxygen revitalizes your body, your mind goes through a resetting phase, and you feel better in your body. There are specific breathing exercises that enable mindfulness. It is not enough to sit somewhere and breathe in and out. Here, you will discover breathing exercises that teach you how to breathe correctly to maximize mindfulness benefits.

Alternate Nostril Breathing

The alternate nostril breathing technique is used during meditation. With this method, you can re-energize your body, mind, and spirit. The steps below will help you maximize this process:

- Use your right thumb to plug your right nostril.

- Using your left nostril, take a deep breath.

- Take off your thumb from the right nostril and plug your left nostril using the ring finger of the same hand.

- Exhale slowly through the left nostril.

- Repeat the process several times then switch, starting with plugging the left nostril...

The Yoga Breathing Technique

The yoga breathing technique is commonly used used during yoga, and it is easy to practice. You can calm your breathing and enjoy mindfulness with this process using the steps below:

- Take a slow breath.
- Take a pause.
- Let your breath out slowly.
- Pause again and repeat the process.

The 4-7-8 Breathing

This is sometimes referred to as the "relaxation method". It is safe to say that this technique is among the easiest ways you can enjoy the mindfulness breathing process. This method can quickly calm your nervous system such that while breathing, you will feel like your nerves are tranquilized. This method is useful for people looking for ways to calm their minds because they suffer from anxiety or sleep disorders. Here is how it works:

- Inhale deeply.
- Place your tongue's tip at the back of your teeth.
- With a whooshing sound and a big sigh, release a deep breath.
- With your mouth closed, inhale through your nose and count to four.
- Hold until the count of seven.
- Exhale deeply and let out a big sigh at the count of eight.
- Repeat the process.

The Count-For-Four Method

The count-for-four technique is common because it is a powerful meditative tool that enables users to count to four and then count backward from four using timed breaths. You can use different numbers (this all depends on your preference), but the count-for-four is the most common, and this is how you can use it:

- Breathe in first – count one
- Breathe out – count two
- Breathe in – count three
- Breathe out – count four
- Breathe in – count three
- Breathe out – count two
- Breathe in – count one
- Breathe out – count two
- Continue to repeat the process at least two or three times.

The Lion's Breath Technique

This mindfulness breathing method is an energizing practice utilized by yoga enthusiasts to eliminate tension in the chest and face. With this method, stress is relieved and pressure ebbs away.

To use this method, you will have to:

- Sit cross-legged in a comfortable place.

- Have your palms pressed against your knees with your fingers spread wide.

- Inhale deeply through your nose with your eyes wide open (just like a lion).

- Open your mouth.

- Stick out your tongue.

- Exhale.

- The muscles in your throat should contract as you exhale through your mouth. Make a loud "HA" sound as you exhale.

- Turn your gaze to consider the space between your eyebrows and the tip of your nose.

- Do this 2-3 times.

Equal Breathing

The equal breathing technique concentrates on helping you inhale and exhale for the same length of time. This enables smooth breathing, steadies your heart rate, and brings about balance and serenity.

To get the best out of this method, you must find a breath length that is just right for you (not too easy and not too hard). Don't breathe too fast and choose a time frame you can maintain (3 to 5 counts is ideal).

After getting used to the breathing process while sitting, you will be able to practice it anytime you need to settle your nerves or get grounded. This technique is done like this:

- Settle into a comfortable position.

- Breathe in and out through your nose.

- Count each inhale and exhale to ensure that the duration of breaths is equal.

- To help with attaining evenness, you can choose a phrase you repeat in your mind while inhaling and exhaling.

- Add a light pause after the inhale and exhale, so you feel comfortable and enjoy the process.

- Continue for five minutes.

Pursed Lips Breathing

The pursed lips breathing technique is one of the simplest ways to slow down your breathing pace and stay in the present moment with each breath. This technique is perfect anytime and can be used multiple times a day.

To practice this method, you should:

- First, relax your neck and shoulders.
- Keep your mouth closed.
- Inhale through your nose slowly for 2 counts.
- Purse your lips.
- Exhale by blowing the air through your pursed lips for a count of 4.
- Repeat a few times until you feel calm.

Resonant or Coherent Breathing

This method is practiced by breathing at a rate of five full breaths per minute, and you can achieve this breathing pace by inhaling and exhaling for a count of five. When you breathe at this rate, your heart rate is maximized, reducing stress and the symptoms of depression.

You can use resonant or coherent breathing by:

- Inhaling for five counts

- Exhaling for five counts

- Repeating the process for a few minutes until you feel a release of tension.

Deep Breathing

With the deep breathing technique, you will experience relief from shortness of breath and feel a deep calm overcome you. With this method, you will breathe in fresh air, thus bringing more oxygen to your brain and body.

While deep breathing in itself is a common breathing technique, doing it through mindfulness is a specific process. You will be taking deep breaths and releasing all anxiety while establishing calm in your body.

To engage in this deep breathing technique, you only have to:

- Stand or sit comfortably and draw your elbows back slightly (this allows your chest to expand when you breathe).

- Inhale deeply through your nose.

- Hold your breath and count to five.

- Release your breath slowly by exhaling through your nose.

- Repeat the process until you feel calm.

This technique brings calm in any situation and will help you reclaim your peace. The secret is to use this breathing intentionally and consistently. More so, you don't have to wait until you are in an "uncomfortable" situation before trying these breathing exercises. Practicing them will help you to feel generally more relaxed and able to handle challenges.

Dedicate space in your schedule a few times a week to practice these breathing techniques. Use them daily to get the maximum benefit. If you want to learn more about breathing exercises, you can speak to a yoga teacher or respiratory therapist. Please check with your doctor if you have medical concerns.

In the next chapter, we will explore meditation as a mindfulness technique.

Chapter Eight: Mindfulness Techniques: Meditation

We have completed the first mindfulness technique, which entailed breathing. Have you been practicing the methods you learned about? There are more methods to explore - methods that will help you get the best out of mindfulness and help you combat fear, worry, and anxiety.

The second technique we will discuss is meditation. It is quite well known and is one of the most discussed methods for practicing mindfulness. This is because of its effectiveness. We will be analyzing meditation and how it aids mindfulness.

Getting caught up in all the activities and tasks you need to do in a day leads to worrying about your capacity and ability to manage your obligations. Through mindful meditation, you get a unique opportunity to pause, take a break from the fast-paced world, and anchor your mind in the present.

Meditation is a mental exercise that entails being FULLY focused in the now by controlling your thoughts, feelings, and sensations without judgment. Mindfulness meditation means controlling yourself mentally, slowing down racing thoughts, letting go of negativity and calming your body and mind.

There are different types of mindfulness techniques, but meditation is a leading method because it is also a combination of other mindfulness techniques. While meditating, you also engage in breathing practices and body awareness, which are two prominent mindfulness techniques. While practicing mindfulness meditation, you don't have to engage in extravagant props and preparations such as scented candles, essential oils, etc.

All you have to do to get started is make some free time, get a comfortable place to sit, set about 3-5 minutes on your timer, and calm your mind to attain a judgment-free mental state. Meditation is all about consistent practice so don't get discouraged if you can't clear your mind and relax the first few times you try. The more you practice, the better you become, and this means it will also become a part of your life. Let's go over the best way to practice mindfulness meditation.

How to Begin

To begin with, you must first recognize that it is a straightforward technique that you can practice on your own. You don't need a teacher or a specific program to get it done unless you practice it for specific health reasons and need assistance with it. Make the decision to do it, and then follow through. The steps below will help get started with the mindfulness meditation process.

Set Time Aside for Meditation

Timing is crucial for active meditation. You must intentionally set time aside for the practice. If you have children at home or around you, you may want to do this 30 minutes before they wake up in the morning, or do it after they go to bed. If you don't have kids, carve out the best time in your day to practice mindfulness meditation. Don't be hard on yourself if you find it hard to make time for your sessions at first, or if you are distracted. Sometimes life gets in the way. Try another time.

Ensure That You Are Comfortable

Next, get relaxed by finding a quiet and comfortable space with minimal or no distractions. You can sit in a chair with your head straight but not stiff, or sit on the floor. Wear comfortable and loose clothes as this helps in keeping you feel free and unconstricted.

Use a Timer

A timer is not compulsory, especially for those used to meditating who can tell when they should start and stop. As a beginner, use a timer or a gentle alarm to focus on meditating without being distracted by the time.

The timer will also help you reduce all excuses for stopping abruptly to do something else. It enables you to meditate for the right amount of time as opposed to worrying that you are there for too long or for too little amount of time.

Concentrate on Your Breathing

When you start meditating, please focus on your breathing pattern and become aware of your breath. Feel your belly rise and fall as the air gets into your nose and leaves your mouth. Also, pay attention to how each breath changes. Focusing on your breathing helps you become mindful of the meditative moment.

Enjoy a Break

While meditating, if you discover that you are getting too distracted or carried away by your thoughts, take a break and bring your mind back to the moment. Sometimes at the initial meditative stages, your mind may wander through thoughts that may incite fear, anxiety or worry. Don't be so hard on yourself if this happens. Instead, focus on practicing how to return to your breathing and refocus on the present through mindfulness.

You Can Use an App

If you struggle with practicing mindfulness meditation on your own, you might want to use apps that provide free meditation sessions and teach you how to stay centered throughout the day. Later, when you are used to getting into a meditative state, you may not need to use these apps.

Practicing mindfulness meditation helps you discover better ways of bringing mindfulness into your everyday life, especially on those very overwhelming days or moments. Using a typical day as an example, you can do a lot of things mindfully and meditatively to attain better control of your mental state and get rid of anxiety.

You are mindful whenever you take a break from work or an activity to focus attention on the present moment. You can ramp this up by being intentional and adding meditation to that mindful process. The mindfulness meditation experience helps you enjoy the present enriching moment rather than being stuck in past failures or future fears.

Here are some simple daily activities you can engage in to help introduce mindfulness meditation to your life:

- While driving, turn on the radio and play soothing music while ensuring your hands are relaxed on the wheel instead of gripping it tightly. Whenever your mind wanders from that moment, bring it back to the song and the road, and stay in that moment.

HOW TO DEAL WITH WORRY AND ANXIETY: SIMPLE MINDFULNESS TECHNIQUES TO RELIEVE STRESS AND FEAR AND LIVE A LIFE WITHOUT DEPRESSION

75

● As you wash the dishes, savor the feeling of the water running through your hands and marvel at the bubbles and the sounds of plates touching each other.

● When brushing your teeth feel your feet on the floor and enjoy the sensation of cleaning your teeth.

● When playing with your kids, enjoy the melody of their laughter. Hold on to the image of them playing and smiling.

These may seem like everyday, regular activities, but they are the best ways to incorporate mindfulness into your life, as they help you stay present. When you meditate, the images and sensations you hold in your memory will become the material that you use to stay grounded in the present.

For example, when you quieten your mind in meditation, you may want to get rid of harmful and toxic thoughts, but this is hard for an idle mind. Focus instead on your memory of the voices of kids laughing, the soothing music as you drove on the highway, or the warm feeling from hugs that grandma gave.

This realization is why mindfulness and meditation are a powerful combination. What you are mindful of ultimately becomes what you meditate on. This is a perfect way of combating anxiety and worry. The primary objective is to make mindfulness meditation a consistent part of your life.

Great! Now that you know how mindfulness meditation works, we will move on to the next technique, which is also very popular and effective. Let's learn about YOGA!!

Chapter Nine: Mindfulness Techniques: Yoga

Yoga is an ancient practice. People rely on it to relieve life's stresses, ease their minds, and find inner peace. While yoga and mindfulness are not novel ideas, the concept of "mindful yoga" is relatively new. Here we will consider how best to utilize this technique for combating anxiety, worry, and fear.

Mindful yoga merges yoga and mindfulness practices to help an individual stay present in the moment while basking in the connection one has with their body, mind, soul, and spirit. Mindfulness is a part of the physical practice of yoga. This idea helps an individual maintain focus on their mind-body by being aware of themselves at a moment in time.

With yoga, your exercises become meditative through mindfulness as you are 100% present instead of engaging in yoga only for the postures and exercises. As a mindfulness technique, yoga holds the promise of helping an individual combat fear through body awareness, heightened spiritual connection, and meditation.

Engaging in mindful awareness while participating in yoga as a physical activity raises your focus level. It becomes difficult for negative thoughts to penetrate your mind and steal your consciousness of the moment.

A crucial aspect of the yoga mindfulness technique is its emphasis on observation rather than reaction. Greater importance is put on observing the content of the mind, feelings, and emotions while in a yoga pose. That observation leads to a better understanding of self as opposed to criticism.

Through this process, you can dig deeper into your subconscious to understand "why" and gain clarity on specific issues.

Mindfulness works in any yoga class, and it can be used with any yoga technique because it contributes to and enhances the consciousness of the moment. The next time you engage in yoga, remember mindful yoga and try to incorporate mindfulness into your techniques. When you do, you will observe that your yoga moments are more effective in helping you combat fear.

Mindful yoga is not as traditional as regular yoga practices because there is less focus on posture and more emphasis on the awareness of the body and mind. While engaging in mindful yoga, you will be encouraged to work mainly within your mind by first learning how to accept yourself with compassion, and how to open up to your life's possibilities.

Some people feel the impact of yoga deeply and strongly while engaged in the practice itself, and afterward, they get back to the same cycle of anxiety and worry because they weren't mindful during their yoga practice. Through mindful yoga, you not only focus on the yoga activity itself but also seek to strike a permanent positive connection between the postures and the impact it has on your mind.

Mindful yoga also helps you listen to your body carefully and intently with sincere honesty. Sometimes, stress spirals over into anxiety because we do not pay enough attention to our bodies and minds. The "fast" life in modern society prompts us to minimize the importance of pausing and paying attention to our body's rhythm.

However, with mindful yoga, you do not only listen to your thoughts. You also become conscious of your body. Body awareness is a mindfulness technique we will discuss in Chapter Ten. Mindful yoga is the process of weaving all the elements of mindfulness and yoga together to attain a holistic, positive experience.

Some of the elements woven together include posture, breath, movement, and body consciousness. With these, you can eliminate pressure from your life and live in the moment.

How to Practice Mindful Yoga

The best way to practice mindful yoga is using a systematic approach of defined steps instead of just being mindful while using yoga postures. This systematic approach means being intentional about your practice. While mindfulness works with different yoga postures, you need to know the poses you will engage in so you are conscious of what you are striving for. It is not enough for you to show up and get started with yoga. As with meditation, you have to be intentional with the practice. You need to make time and pay attention to getting the most out of your activity.

Yoga Body Scans

Body scans enhance mindful yoga. This requires you to seek areas of your body that need attention and engage in yoga postures that focus on those areas. While working on this physical aspect of your body, you will also align your thoughts and senses, such that your energies are harmonized for effective change.

With mindful yoga, you are encouraged to become curious and open with body exploration, which prompts you to effect physical changes through mental connection. For example, a symptom of fear in your life is a faster heart rate, which can be unhealthy as it can lead to tachycardia, which is a high heart rate. If the heart rate continues at a high level, it can lead to a heart attack.

Through mindful yoga using body scan, you can become conscious of physical issues caused by a mental strain and calm your heart rate as you focus on your breathing.

Yoga Instructions

Mindful yoga can be maximized through yoga instruction if the individual is working with a yoga instructor. After yoga students get into their initial posture, they should be reminded to become mindful by first focusing on their breath. Is the breath deep? Slow? Fast? Shallow?

Mindfulness activated during such sessions focuses on where the sensation arises from in the body. It is also about how present the individual is at that moment. If the yoga class is a group activity, students have to avoid being distracted by looking at other participants.

The yoga instructions are also crucial to ensuring harmony between breathing, body awareness, posture, and consciousness of the moment. The instructor should remind the participants to come back to the present moment and become aware of what is happening around them. Through this reminder, students will identify disturbing thoughts, understand why they feel that way, and come to terms with the issues instead of running away from them.

Yoga and the Four Foundations of Mindfulness

Mindful yoga through the "four foundations of mindfulness" involves the following:

- **Mindfulness of the body:** We will discuss body consciousness and awareness in another chapter, but before getting to that, you should know that being mindful of your body is crucial during mindful yoga. You will be using your body during yoga postures, but there is also a connection between your body, mind, soul, and spirit. While being mindful of your mind, thoughts and feelings, pay attention to your body movements.

- **Mindfulness of mind:** Mindfulness of the mind empowers the individual to stay connected to the mind and its contents such that you don't lose control of your thoughts. You only keep the good and discard the toxic. More so, mindfulness of the mind during yoga helps you understand that WE ARE NOT OUR THOUGHTS! You may have unpleasant thoughts sometimes because you've had unpleasant circumstances, but that doesn't mean you are a nasty person. Mindful yoga helps you with this distinction.

- **Mindfulness of feelings:** Mindfulness of feelings refers to bodily sensations and emotions and labeling them as pleasant or unpleasant. When engaged in mindful yoga, you will quickly know a pleasant warmth and hold on to it, while discovering uncomfortable emotions and letting them go.

To get the best out of mindfulness and deal with anxiety and worry, you must be intentional with mindful yoga. Yes, yoga is excellent, but mindful yoga is an enhanced way of maintaining a connection with all aspects of your life such that there is no room for negativity.

In the next chapter, let's talk about the last mindfulness technique which focuses on body awareness!!!

Chapter Ten: Mindfulness Techniques: Body Awareness

Lastly, we will talk about body awareness. It is one of the most crucial mindfulness techniques you can use to deal with worry and anxiety. Body awareness is the ability to be conscious of everything that relates to your body. Why is it so important? Body awareness helps us understand how to connect with ourselves, other people, and our environment.

From birth, through childhood and into adulthood, we are raised to be conscious of what happens around us. This training makes us focus our attention on what happens to us and around us instead of what happens within us. The problem with having a lack of body awareness is that you don't know your anxiety triggers, and you won't know how to respond when you experience such physical triggers.

By using body awareness as a mindfulness technique you still notice what happens around you, but your first commitment is to your body and being conscious about the connection between your emotions and your body.

Right now, as you read this book, how you feel? How does your body feel? Are you conscious of the impact your emotions have over your body? When we talk about dealing with fear, anxiety and worry, we often ignore the physical aspects, but your body is just as important as your mind.

Body awareness is also related to the concept of body management, which is the capacity to identify and integrate information from your senses. Your body is always speaking, but the question is, "Are you listening?" Before your body breaks down from fear, worry, and anxiety, it will have given you indicators that it was in distress. Did you ignore them?

Some of the indicators may be attributed to stress, pressure from others or the pain of unfulfilled expectations that leads to sleepless nights. Whatever the triggers may be, the body always gives hints, but when people are extremely busy and are not MINDFUL of their bodies, they miss such clues.

However, with body awareness and intentional mindfulness, you will check in on yourself regularly to take stock of your body's state and how you feel. Using this technique, you can reduce tension, combat fear, and increase your motor awareness.

Fear, anxiety, worry, and all other negative emotions have a significant impact on our bodies. When you become intentional with body awareness, you bring attention to your physical state and are able to combat these feelings more effectively. Everything about mindful body awareness is practical, as you will discover through the steps below.

Get Comfortable

Start the body awareness practice by getting comfortable. Sit upright on a seat or sit cross-legged on the floor. Point the top of your head straight to the ceiling, and rest your hands on your legs, either face down or face up, whatever is most comfortable.

Close Your Eyes

Next, close your eyes gently and focus on your body by leaving the outside world out and keeping your thoughts away from it. Then, focus on your breathing. Inhale and exhale deeply and evenly while filling your belly with breath. Concentrate on your breathing and pay attention to your body by noticing how your hands, legs, and other body parts feel.

Maintain Your Attention

Pay attention to your entire body by noticing everything from your head to your toes and then move your toes so you can feel them. Imagine your breath moving from your chest to your legs, feet, and into all your toes. Sometimes we ignore our feet, forgetting that they take us everywhere and can get quickly tired. Through this body awareness experience, you can wake your feet up and give them life again.

Focus on Your Body Parts

Next, you can focus on other body parts one by one, and notice your heart rate and how rhythmic it is. Let your breath move up from your toes, past your knees, fill up your belly with air, and then proceed back to your chest. Check how it feels. Do you think you have a standard or abnormal heart rate? Do you feel at ease, or disturbed? Become more conscious of your arms and shoulders. If you are tense, your joints will be stiff, and you need to release such tension by breathing in and releasing the air while letting your shoulders down. Let your breath move to the neck area and into your head. If you feel thoughts seeping into your head, breathe them out and float them away. Then slowly allow the breath to return to your belly and slowly open your eyes as you let the air out from your mouth.

Body Awareness Through Visualization

You can become fully aware of your body's tension and release it through the visualization process:

● Lie or sit down in a relaxed position, get comfortable and close your eyes.

● Breathe in thoroughly and slowly, allowing your breathing to pass through your mind over your body while sensing every part without thinking about it.

● While breathing, seek out areas of tension, pain, or discomfort and analyze such feelings in your body.

● Ask yourself, "Why does my headache? Why is there tension in my scalp? Are my shoulders tight? Is my heart racing? Do I feel flushed?"

● By answering the questions above, you will locate places where you feel such discomfort and ascertain why you feel that way.

● Visualization comes by inhaling, and while exhaling, you visualize the breath passing over your body, healing those parts that have stress, tension, and discomfort. The parts where you feel pain should receive the most attention as you work with your mind to relax your body.

● With full breaths, pull the air into your body to establish calm and peace such that your body finds release while you visualize healing.

● With five slow breaths, count back to the present moment and stay calm after the fifth breath. Open your eyes and remain still before moving from that spot.

What do you think about the body awareness technique? It's great, right? Well, you can only master the process when you do it intentionally and repeatedly. Even if you don't get it right at the first try, don't give up.

The steps highlighted above apply whenever you want to take some time to engage in intentional body awareness like you would do with yoga or meditation sessions. A quiet place to engage in mindful body awareness is helpful, but you can also do a modified version of it as you carry on with your daily activities. So, if you are extremely busy and cannot give time and attention to dedicated body awareness sessions as often as you want to, then you can engage in the technique while on the move.

For example, if you fly around a lot, you can easily practice body awareness while on the aircraft, especially if you notice that you are really stressed. When anxiety is beginning to creep into your mind, unsettling your body, take a few minutes to pay attention to your body using the tips shared with you in this chapter.

Similarly, if you are in a car or waiting to pick up your child from school, you could use those few minutes to practice body awareness. Check on yourself and ensure you are in a healthy and peaceful state. All body awareness exercises relieve stress and help you become more mindful of how your body reacts to external impacts from people, places, and things.

Body awareness as a mindfulness technique also strengthens the connection between your body and mind such that you can easily modulate the flow of ideas and how they affect your body. If you always feel uneasy in your body when you are around a particular person, such that you start to sweat nervously, have an increased heartbeat, and sometimes feel headaches, then maybe that person is toxic.

If you don't manage the relationship you have with that person, or if you don't find ways to avoid meeting them, that uncomfortable feeling may develop into fear and anxiety. With the body awareness technique, you can ease the tension caused by such a person's effect on your body and prevent them from affecting your emotional state.

With this chapter on using body awareness as a mindfulness technique, we have come to the end of the book's chapters on techniques and are ready to move on to the last part. The next chapter highlights tips, concepts, and ideas about how you can incorporate mindfulness into your daily life. As much as we have discovered the importance of mindfulness, we need to learn how to apply it to everyday experiences.

Chapter Eleven: Incorporating Mindful Practices Into Your Daily Life

Some people hear the term "mindfulness" and instantly think it is a complicated process that entails very "serious" activities which are only for truly dedicated individuals. However, from all you have learned thus far, I believe you know better and understand that mindfulness has nothing to do with complicated processes.

You can incorporate mindfulness into your daily routines, and it is possible to make the techniques a part of your life, but this requires commitment and intentionality. Some people are incredibly passive about mindfulness because they are always seeking a particular time to do it "right", but waiting for such "special" moments only encourages procrastination.

You can become mindful and maximize the techniques even at this moment as you read. You can pay attention to the present moment and become more conscious of the events in your life, but you need to do it actively and be aware of what you do.

For example, if you are going to meditate, do just that. Don't close your eyes and open them after a few seconds and call that meditation. You need to know that "Yes, now I am about to meditate, or now I am about to engage in yoga." When you are intentional with mindfulness techniques, you will easily incorporate them into your life and enjoy the process.

Natural Ways of Being Mindful Every Day

Below are natural ways to practice being mindful.

Practice Mindfulness as You Wait

One of the key things you should remember from this book is that every opportunity to practice mindfulness is significant, and waiting is one such opportunity. If you are in an office waiting to speak with someone else, don't just sit there, allowing negative thoughts to gather.

Take control of your mind when it wanders off towards negative thoughts by being mindful of your mind's content. In a waiting room, parked in your car, at the park, or in any lineup, you can meditate, use breathing techniques or practice body awareness to stay calm.

Use Mindfulness While in Transit

During your day, you may have to travel from one place to another, and you can incorporate mindfulness during those times. While in transit, you can take as many seconds or minutes you have available to become conscious and increasingly aware of your body and mind. This is especially easy if you are on public transit. When driving a car, always concentrate on driving!

Use Mindfulness When You Wake Up

Another great way of practicing mindfulness and incorporating it into your daily activity is waking up in the morning using one of the techniques. The meditation mindfulness technique is suited as a morning ritual that helps you kick-start your day on a high note. Some people worry before sleeping and wake up anxious and just stumble into their day without doing anything to help themselves, like meditating.

Using mindfulness techniques such as body awareness, meditation, and yoga will help you to stay calm and start your day in an empowered mental state.

Practice Mindfulness While Engaged In Daily Routine Activities

You can also practice mindfulness while involved in daily activities and routines such as cooking, cleaning, playing with the kids, or even visiting friends. Always engage consciously with whatever you may be doing and be fully present in all social contexts. If you are in a friend's home physically for a visit, be there and not somewhere else in your mind.

Mindful Eating

Some people eat a whole meal without being conscious of the act of consuming food. It is just a necessity that they fulfill. You can incorporate mindfulness into your daily routine through eating with thought and purpose. The next time you get a plate of food, turn it into a more satisfying experience by eating mindfully. First, savor the aroma of the meal, be conscious of each spoonful, and feel the tingle of your taste buds when you put it into your mouth.

Slow down while chewing and experience the rich flavor of the food. This offers the promise of a more enriching food consumption experience compared to rushing through the meal. You may wonder how this aids in combating anxiety. Through mindful eating, you will derive greater joy and satisfaction with each eating experience and be happier. Is a happy person an anxious one? Absolutely not!!

Mindful Relationship Conversations

Every day we converse and interact with different people in our lives based on the kind of relationship we have with them. From interactions with spouses, kids, bosses, employees, close friends, etc. to people we just see at the grocery store, these relationships affect our mindset.

You can incorporate mindfulness into your relationship conversations by being present when discussing things with the people in your life. Listen to understand and hold the memories of such moments in your mind.

The words you hear and the people in your life contribute to helping you maintain a positive or negative disposition. For example, if you are not mindful of the kind of conversations you have with friends, you may be exposed to negative words that cause you to worry all the time. But through mindfulness, you will have better control over what you receive and what you give to such relationship conversations.

Mindfulness Workout

Whatever your physical activities may be, you can incorporate mindfulness by being conscious and present during such activities. Mindful exercise can be done when you take an early morning walk in the neighborhood or use the treadmill. Regardless of what it may be, be present!

You can synchronize your body, mind, and nervous system through mindful workouts, and unlike when you use to work out without being aware, this process helps you enjoy the experience and bask in that moment.

This final chapter aims to empower you with information about how to incorporate all the information you've learned into your daily experiences. Most of the time, people become excited at the prospect of learning how to combat fear and deal with anxiety, but right after dealing with their immediate issues, they forget to maintain the process.

Please note that mindfulness techniques are not solely meant for the horrible times you have to deal with issues. While they are effective in helping you deal with negative events, you should also make mindfulness techniques a part of your daily routine. If you incorporate mindfulness fully into your routine, you won't have to "deal" with anxiety, worry, and fear because you will always be in excellent mental, emotional, physical, and psychological shape.

Final Words

Indeed, worries and doubts are part of everyone's normal life. It's easy to start worrying when you are yet to see your final marks, have an unpaid bill, an upcoming job interview, are starting a new job, or even going on a date with someone. This is normal.

However, when the worry is excessive and becomes uncontrollable, that is beyond normal. If you keep worrying about the "what ifs" of life, or the bad things that may happen, and you can't keep anxious thoughts out of your head, it will surely interfere with your daily life and affect you negatively.

Keeping negative thoughts in your head and constantly worrying will take a toll on both your physical and emotional health. It will drain off your emotional energy, leaving you with headaches, muscle tension, stomach problems, insomnia, and loss of concentration. This negative feeling may radiate, and you will start taking it out on people around you. It may even get worse and you start doing drugs, alcohol, or self-medicating. These are vices that can be avoided.

If you are plagued with anxiety and worry, I hope this book has given you faith that there is a way to improve your circumstance. I also hope I have taught you how to combat your fears and anxiety by using simple mindfulness techniques.

I know how frightening uncertainty can be, especially when there is a need to protect yourself from the unknown. Since you can't predict what is to come, it is important to find ways to cope with the thoughts so that they won't be a problem in your life. You can train your mind and brain to remain

HOW TO DEAL WITH WORRY AND ANXIETY: SIMPLE MINDFULNESS TECHNIQUES TO RELIEVE STRESS AND FEAR AND LIVE A LIFE WITHOUT DEPRESSION

103

calm while looking at life with less fear and a more balanced perspective.

Anxiety and chronic worrying is a mental habit that you can break free from. By deciding to read this book, you've shown that you are ready to break free from the chain of anxiety and worry. By reading up to this very point you've shown how dedicated and ready you are to make change in your life. I must commend you for staying with me all the way through!

Your life is what you make of it, regardless of what happens around you. It is your responsibility to ensure that you are surrounded by positive energy. It is a given that life is not perfect. Life is not always a bed of roses, but that doesn't mean it has to be a bed of thorns. Anxiety, depression, worry, and all other negative energies are thorns. Throughout this book, we have highlighted significant mindfulness techniques that will help you turn those thorns into peaceful experiences.

We kick-started our journey with insight on the definition of anxiety as a foundational concept and built on that idea with Chapter Two detailing anxiety risk factors. The symptoms of anxiety were extensively discussed even as we considered the idea of mindfulness, its benefits, and how to use the techniques.

From breathing exercises to meditation, yoga, and body awareness, you unearthed different ways to maximize mindfulness. Finally, we rounded off the learning curve with a chapter on how to incorporate mindfulness practice into your daily life because execution really matters.

Talking about execution, you must understand that all you have learned can only become valuable and impactful when you utilize the techniques. This is the central reason for the practical and applicable final chapter in this book. When we discover transformative ideas with the potential to change our trajectory, we must intentionally maximize the chance to make the concepts work for us.

Now you know the truth about how to deal with anxiety and worry. You now know that mindfulness is the most effective tool to use to change your story, but knowing this is not enough. What is the value of knowing how to prepare a delicious meal if you don't try to make it and eat it? You have received so much information in the pages of this book that now is the time to take action.

The only way you can truly ascertain if mindfulness works is to use the practices and techniques you've learned. So, from this moment forward, start creating plans for how you can enjoy mindfulness through breathing exercises, meditation, yoga, and body awareness.

As you use these techniques, it will become easier for you to make them a part of your life such that you no longer have to "think" about meditating or body awareness. You do it because it is a routine. Gradually, you will observe significant changes in your life regarding worry and anxiety. As opposed to always being worried and anxious, you will live a more peaceful life.

Some people enjoy that peace only for a brief moment because they execute the ideas relating to mindfulness but fail to SUSTAIN the process. Think about this: Is it possible to lose weight by exercising and eating healthy meals only once every month? Of course not! You must apply yourself everyday to accomplish the betterment of your body. Similarly, you will not find peace and calm and conquer worry and anxiety if you do not apply yourself to the task daily.

As we round off this experience together, I urge you to **remember** all you've read, **act** on the ideas and **sustain** the process. This is how you keep worry and anxiety at bay and out of your life for good.

Best wishes!